THE CHRISTIAN MARRIAGE COUNSELING WORKBOOK

Marriage the Way God Created It

Dustin A. Largent

Dedication

For my wife, Julie who has been with me for better or for worse, for richer or poorer, in sickness and in health and whom I choose to love each day. Thank you for all your love and support.

CONTENTS

Congratulations on your engagement. Marriage is not only one of the greatest gifts God gives us, but it is one of the first gifts given to man. In the garden, God said, "It is not good for the man to be alone. I will make a helper suitable for him."[1]

A man and woman coming together in the covenant of marriage is God's idea. God thought of marriage and God created marriage. Even more, God created it exactly the way he wanted it. His plan for marriage, guidelines for marriage, blessings for marriage and His restrictions upon it are all perfect as they are given to us from God. Unfortunately, there are many who think they are smarter than God and believe they can take something created by an omniscient and omnipotent God and make it better. The arrogance is astounding.

By way of introduction, I want you to get this concept in your head and embrace it. Marriage is a gift from

God to be entered into and lived God's way. God defined marriage. If you recreate it in your own image, your marriage will never measure up to the blessing a marriage, according to God's definition, can be. If you want to change the rules of marriage, your marriage will fall infinitely short of the blessing that marriage, according to God's guidelines, will provide. Should you decide that marriage, according to the Christian Bible, is too restrictive in our enlightened contemporary world, I suggest you prepare for a life void of the love and happiness that marriage on God's terms provides.

God's intention is for your marriage partner to be a lifelong gift that will bring you joy and support until you return to him at death. We don't get to define the gifts we receive from God. We don't get to customize them according to our liking. Remember that marriage was birthed in the infinite wisdom of God. If you embrace this gift as it has been given, without redefining it according to your own desires, you will enjoy the true blessing that is marriage.

MARRIAGE DEFINED

We see marriage for the first time in the second chapter of Genesis. The passage is as follows,

But for Adam no suitable helper was found. [21] So the LORD God caused the man to fall into a deep sleep; and while he was sleeping, he took one of the man's ribs and closed up the place with flesh. [22] Then the LORD God made a woman from the rib he had taken out of the man, and he brought her to the man. [23] The man said, "This is now bone of my bones and flesh of my flesh; she shall be called, woman, for she was taken out of me." [24] For this reason a man will leave his father and mother and be united to his wife, and they will become one flesh. [25] The man and his wife were both naked, and they felt no shame."[2]

This passage gives us the purpose for marriage. It says there was not a suitable helper for Adam. Apparently, God believes that we shouldn't "go it alone". But wasn't God in the garden with Adam? Apparently, though God was present with Adam in the garden, he was still alone without a companion. In Genesis 2:18, God says, *"It is not good for the man to be alone. I will make a helper suitable for him."*[3] It would be fair to say that not only are men better off with a helper, but women fair better as well. What a man and woman need from their helper, however, seems to differ greatly. For instance, it is commonly known that though a man's primary need from his wife is to be respected, a woman's primary need from her husband is to be loved.

The suitable helper that God made for Adam was a woman. Here, we see marriage clearly defined as between a man and a woman. The reason God did not create another man for Adam was because a man would not be a suitable helper. In addition, two men would not be able to populate the world.

Though this may seem obvious, cultures and governments have taken it upon themselves to redefine marriage in a way that accommodates their own image of what a marriage should look like and how it should be defined. The relatively recent shift in definition and purpose of marriage finds its roots, not in a Biblical or historical foundation, but rather in a progressive push to eliminate absolute truth with relative truth. In other words, the once clear lines of morality, rightness, wrongness, and the definitions that went with them, are now being based on the feelings and desires of the individual, rather than Biblical, historical or objective truth. Marriage is no longer defined in the United States and other western countries by going back to its initial Creator and His initial purpose. Instead, we have redefined marriage to accommodate our own desires, preferences, ideas of fairness and individual purposes.

> Instead of erasing the history of marriage and redefining it to fit our own desires and wants, consider taking marriage for what it is and has been for thousands of years. Accept marriage as it is defined by God with all its purposes and benefits.

This will not do. God created marriage according to His infinite wisdom and for His own purposes. God declared that men should marry women and women should marry men. Pairing men with women directly corresponds with God's command to the first man and woman to be fruitful and multiply. This is not to say that married couples must procreate, but rather to illustrate that one of the primary blessings of marriage is naturally eliminated when the Biblical marriage of a man and a woman is abandoned and redefined.

The natural rebuttal to this line of thinking is to progress even further and take procreation, and sex for that matter, out of the confines of marriage. If sex is no longer restricted to marriage, understanding that procreation is a natural result of sex, we seemingly eliminate the argument against same sex marriage. In the process, however, we also destroy marriage as we know it. Monogamy in marriage is undermined and children are born outside of loving married family units.

There is a better way. It's a simpler way as well. Instead of erasing the history of marriage and redefining it to fit our own desires and wants, consider taking marriage for what it is and has been for thousands of years. Accept marriage as it is defined by God with all its purposes and benefits. If I put my dog in a three-piece suit and call him Robert, I haven't miraculously changed the dog into a person. All I've done is try to redefine something without really changing what it is. Marriage will continue to be a lifelong pledge and commitment between a man and a woman, and my dressed-up dog will still not really be a human being.

COUPLE DISCUSSION QUESTIONS

Take some time to talk through the following questions. Allow equal time for both of you to talk and listen.

1) Read Genesis 2:18-25.

2) What do you think makes a helper suitable?

3) Vs. 9- Why were the animals not suitable helpers, when pets make great companions?

4) What do you believe is the definition of marriage?

5) How have you seen the cultural definition of marriage change over the past 10 years?

6) Have the changes to the definition of marriage resulted from God changing or from culture changing?

7) Do you agree with your fiancé about what a marriage is? Do you agree with God?

8) Other than being a lifelong commitment, what other attributes of a marriage are distinct and important?

MOVING OUT TOGETHER

Men often complain about how difficult it is to understand women. They speak of them as if they are from another planet and are beyond understanding. Truly there are many differences both physically and emotionally between men and women, but verse 23 states that the woman is *"bone of my bones and flesh of my flesh"*. In other words, though we may have many differences, we are basically sewn from the same cloth. Be encouraged that you can understand this person that will be one flesh with you. According to scripture, the intimacy between a man and women is unparalleled. In the Biblical story of creation, the woman is taken from the flesh of man when God fashions her from Adam's rib. Later, we find that when a man and woman marry, the two again become one flesh. It's as if the flesh Adam gave up for creating Eve returns to him upon marriage.

In verse 24, it says that a man will leave his father and mother and be united to his wife.[4] There is great wisdom here and an important concept to understand and apply. Before marrying, you must be willing to leave mom and dad. Your relationship with your parents is and should be inherently changed when you get married. Men will continue to be sons and women will continue to be daughters, however the place of those relationships will and should be outranked by the new spousal relationship. For you men, your mommy is no longer the primary woman in your life. For you women, your husband is now the primary man in your life. Certainly, we must continue to love and respect our parents and hopefully, they will be a great source of love, support, and encouragement for you as a couple. However, it's important to understand that entering a marriage relationship fundamentally changes prior roles.

When you became a Christian by entering a committed relationship with Jesus, it fundamentally changed other relationships. It changed who held authority in your life. It changed where you went for primary wisdom and direction. Your primary purpose of living to please yourself or please your parents and friends is usurped by this new relationship with Jesus, causing your decisions, worldview, and resulting actions to change. We will still listen and respect the opinions of others, but ultimately the Word of God trumps all others.

In a similar way, your marriage should change the order of importance in your familial relationships. The order before marriage may have been God, then parents, then yourself followed by friends. Once married, the correct order is God, then spouse, then everything else.

> . . . a man will LEAVE his father and mother. One of the reasons this is important is that a man must establish himself as the leader of his family. This is something virtually impossible to do while living under his or her daddy's roof.

With this shift in relationship, being fundamental to the marriage relationship, living arrangements once married are important for establishing those roles. Sometimes couples get married and immediately move in with their parents or their in-laws. Often the plan is to save money for a down-payment on a house or to pay off student loans. Though ancient Jewish grooms would prepare a place for their bride by building a new house onto his father's existing home[42], it was still his own household. As more generations got married and new homes were built on the old one, a housing complex was created called an insula.[42] He didn't move his bride into his old bedroom and continue to have mom make his bed. Though he is still in close proximity to his father and mother, Ephesians 5:31 remains true, *"For this reason a man will leave his father and mother and be united to his wife, and the two will become one flesh."* I would suggest, those planning to get married and continue to live at home with mom and dad really reconsider.

It says that a man will *leave* his father and mother. One of the reasons this is important is that a man must establish himself as the leader of his family. This is something virtually impossible to do while living under his or her daddy's roof. When you live under your parent's roof, you continue to live under the ultimate authority of your parents. The necessary change in relationship roles is stagnated because one of the newly married is still living at home with his or her parents. For this reason, if you are unable to leave home because you can't do it financially, you probably aren't financially ready to get married.

Marriage must be entered into on God's terms as He has defined it in scripture. It shows us that a man should leave home and be with his wife as the head of a new household. Finally, there is an unparalleled intimacy available to men and women represented by the return of the woman to the man as they again become one flesh.

COUPLE DISCUSSION QUESTIONS

Take some time to discuss the following questions. Allow equal time for both of you to talk and listen.

1) Talk about your current relationship with your father.

2) Talk about your current relationship with your mother.

3) How have these relationships formed your views, opinions, and decision making until now?

4) In what ways do you believe these relationships will change once you are married?

5) What expectations do you have of your fiancé regarding the relationship with your future in-laws and your parents?

6) Are we in a position financially to be independent or are we still dependent on our parents?

7) What will your living arrangements be once you are married and how will this foster appropriate roles as husband, wife, son, daughter, son-in-law, etc?

8) What current aspects of our relationships with our parents will we continue to encourage and foster?

JESUS AND THE CHURCH

We can't have a discussion of marriage without taking a good look at the relationship Jesus has with the church. Scripture makes numerous comparisons between earthly marriage and the relationship Christ has with His church. By exploring these passages, we can come to a better understanding of what a true marriage should look like.

The Biblical passages that reference marriage assume we have some understanding of first century Jewish marriage customs. To be better equipped to understand these passages, let's take a quick look at betrothal and marriage during the first century.

Brides were traditionally chosen for a groom by the groom's father by considering carefully the family of the bride and her lineage.[5] The groom and his father would go to the father of the bride and a bride price would be established and paid to the father of the bride.[5] Interestingly, a wine ceremony would then be performed where the bride and groom would sit at a table facing each other.[5] The groom would then take the cup of wine and hold it up saying, "This cup is a new covenant in my blood, which I offer to you."[5] No Christian who has read the Bible would fail to recognize these words spoken by the groom in the wine ceremony. These words are strikingly similar to the words spoken by Jesus when He shared the cup with His disciples at the last supper. Luke 22:20 reads,

In the same way, after the supper he took the cup, saying, "This cup is the new covenant in my blood, which is poured out for you.[6]

This reveals that Jesus really does view the church as his bride. Like the weddings of the first century, the marriage of Christ to the church is an arranged marriage. God has selected the church to be Christ's bride. We did not choose God, but God chose us. Furthermore, the church is not a bride that can be gained easily. The bride price for the church is costly because the bride comes with great debt. Some of you are considering marrying someone who has a bunch of student loan debt or credit card debt. The bride of Christ comes with a debt of sin. Romans 6:23 says,

For the wages of sin is death, but the gift of God is

eternal life in Christ Jesus our Lord.[7]

Jesus pays the bride price for the church with His own death. Christ's death on the cross was payment for the debt of His bride.

Paul says,

[25] Husbands, love your wives, just as Christ loved the church and gave himself up for her [26] to make her holy, cleansing her by the washing with water through the word, [27] and to present her to himself as a radiant church, without stain or wrinkle or any other blemish, but holy and blameless.[8]

Scripture teaches us that Jesus gave Himself up. This means he surrendered His life, for the church to purify her. He does this so that He can marry a pure and holy bride. Like most men, Jesus wants a bride who is holy and pure. When the bride puts on that white wedding dress, she should think about the *"radiant church, without stain or wrinkle or any other blemish, but holy and blameless."[9]*

It never ceases to amaze me, the cost of a white wedding dress. It's a dress that a woman will only wear for one day, yet women pay thousands of dollars for the perfect dress. From a symbolic standpoint, the cost for the church to wear all white (be pure and spotless on her wedding day) is more costly still. It cost the groom His life. Christ's sacrifice on the cross is the only way His bride (the church) can stand spotless and pure before Him.

The couple would be betrothed to one another once the cup of wine is passed back to the groom, and he drinks from the cup.[5] The engagement is as binding as if they were married.[5] We see this play out when we read the Christmas story of Mary and Joseph. In the first chapter of Matthew, we read:

[18] *This is how the birth of Jesus the Messiah came about: His mother Mary was pledged to be married to Joseph, but before they came together, she was found to be pregnant through the Holy Spirit.* [19] *Because Joseph her husband was faithful to the law, and yet did not want to expose her to public disgrace, he had in mind to divorce her quietly.*[10]

In this passage we see that though they were only pledged to be married (we would call them engaged), Joseph is called her husband and he is unable to simply call off the engagement. He would have to divorce her.

The groom would promise to build a place for him to live with his new bride; often an addition to his parent's house.[5] The groom would be gone for up to twelve months before returning to get his bride.[11] This too, is demonstrated by Jesus in His relationship with the church. In John 14 we read:

My Father's house has many rooms; if that were not so, would I have told you that I am going there to prepare a place for you? [3] *And if I go and prepare a place for you, I will come back and take you to be with me that you also may be where I am.[12]*

Jesus has left His bride, the church, to prepare a place for her just as a good first century groom would do. We can rest assured that our groom will return for us in due time.

When the groom returned, it would often be at night at around midnight.[11] We see a parable about the return of Christ in Matthew 25.

"At that time the kingdom of heaven will be like ten virgins who took their lamps and went out to meet the bridegroom. [2] Five of them were foolish and five were wise. [3] The foolish ones took their lamps but did not take any oil with them. [4] The wise ones, however, took oil in jars along with their lamps. [5] The bridegroom was a long time in coming, and they all became drowsy and fell asleep. [6] "At midnight the cry rang out: 'Here's the bridegroom! Come out to meet him!' [7] "Then all the virgins woke up and trimmed their lamps. [8] The foolish ones said to the wise, 'Give us some of your oil; our lamps are going out.' [9] "'No,' they replied, 'there may not be enough for both us and you. Instead, go to those who sell oil and buy some for yourselves. [10] "But while they were on their way to buy the oil, the bridegroom arrived. The virgins who were ready went in with him to the wedding banquet. And the door was shut. [11] "Later the others also came. 'Lord, Lord,' they said, 'open the door for

us!' [12] "But he replied, 'Truly I tell you, I don't know you. [13] "Therefore keep watch, because you do not know the day or the hour.[13] "

It is significant that the virgins did not know exactly when the groom would return. Likewise, the church does not know the day or hour when Christ will return. Matthew 24:36 says,

But about that day or hour no one knows, not even the angels in heaven, nor the Son, but only the Father.[14]

From a symbolic standpoint, the cost for the church to wear all white (be pure and spotless on her wedding day) is more costly still. It cost the groom His life. Christ's sacrifice on the cross is the only way His bride (the church) can stand spotless and pure before Him.

Upon returning, the groom would take the bride to a bridal chamber where they would spend seven days alone.[11]After the seven days, they would join all their guests for a marriage feast where there would be music and dancing.[11] It makes me chuckle, that many churches today still do not allow dancing in their buildings even though first century weddings commonly involved music and dancing.[11]

We get to witness the great wedding feast of Jesus with his church as recorded in Revelation chapter 19:

[6] Then I heard what sounded like a great multitude, like the roar of rushing waters and like loud peals of thunder, shouting.
"Hallelujah!

For our Lord God Almighty reigns. [7] Let us rejoice and be glad and give him glory!
For the wedding of the Lamb has come, and his bride has made herself ready. [8] Fine linen, bright and clean, was given her to wear."

(Fine linen stands for the righteous acts of God's holy people.)

[9] Then the angel said to me, "Write this: Blessed are those who are invited to the wedding supper of the Lamb!" And he added, "These are the true words of God."[5]

As you anticipate marriage and navigate the engagement process, it is clear engagement and marriage are about much more than just two people coming together. As an institution, marriage is not some man-made agreement between two people committing to each other for a certain amount of time. Indeed, marriage has roots and meanings deeper than any individual couple. Marriage points to more than a couple's future. It points to the Creator of marriage. It points to the relationship between Christ and His church. In Christ and the church, is a demonstration of how to be a husband and wife. In the next chapter we will look at what this means from a practical standpoint.

COUPLE DISCUSSION QUESTIONS

Take some time to talk through the following questions. Allow equal time for both of you to talk and listen.

1) What surprised you about first century weddings?

2) Are there any aspects of first century weddings that you wish we still implemented today?

3) What are some aspects of Christ's relationship with the church that can be applied to your relationship with your fiancé or spouse?

4) Does the relationship between Christ and the church show us anything about the roles of husbands and wives?

5) How does Christ show His love for the church and how is the church to show love to Christ?

6) How long does the marriage relationship between Christ and the church last?

INSIGHTS FROM JESUS AND THE CHURCH

There are a few obvious observations that we can draw from a broad look at Christ's relationship with the church. First, there is only one Biblical church. Though the church is composed of many denominations around the world, there is truly only one church made up of all people who have been saved through Jesus. Scripture is also clear that there is only one God. The model for marriage is one Christ and one Church. There are not multiple churches in this relationship, nor are there multiple Gods. In fact, God is adamant in the Old Testament that we shouldn't have other Gods. This is the very first commandment.

You shall have no other gods before me.[27]

As I discussed in chapter 1, a biblically defined marriage

is between only two people. If you watch television, you will see shows about polygamous marriages. Perhaps you've caught an episode of the show Sister Wives or some other reality show involving polygamy. One of the reasons people are entertained by these shows is our fascination with train wrecks. We like to peak into all the problems caused by one guy having multiple wives. You will even find examples of polygamists in scripture, but just because polygamy is present in scripture doesn't make it God's plan. You may recall a bunch of Israelites fashioning a golden calf in scripture too, but I don't remember that action drawing heavenly applause. God's plan is for one man to marry one woman.

You will also notice that Jesus and the church are very different. Jesus doesn't decide to marry another God like himself. The Christian church should not abandon Christ and choose to be united with other earthly churches. Though the issue is sensitive in today's culture, marriage was intended to be between one man and one woman. This is confirmed by every married couple we see in scripture as well as the relationship Christ has with the church. In Genesis, we read of the creation of mankind:

So God created mankind in his own image, in the image of God he created them; male and female he created them.[28] God blessed them and said to them, "Be fruitful and increase in number; fill the earth and subdue it. Rule over the fish in the sea and the birds in the sky and over every living creature that moves on the ground."28

Again, part of our role as a married couple is to increase in number. In other words, get pregnant and have babies. This doesn't mean all couples have to have children, but the model of a married couple is one that by design can produce fruit (children).

Though homosexual marriage is becoming widely acceptable in society today, it simply doesn't conform to the Biblical model of marriage. In addition, God can not approve of marriage in a relationship type that He considers sinful. In the first chapter of Romans, we read:

[24] Therefore God gave them over in the sinful desires of their hearts to sexual impurity for the degrading of their bodies with one another. [25] They exchanged the truth about God for a lie, and worshiped and served created things rather than the Creator— who is forever praised. Amen. [26] Because of this, God gave them over to shameful lusts. Even their women exchanged natural sexual relations for unnatural ones. [27] In the same way the men also abandoned natural relations with women and were inflamed with lust for one another. Men committed shameful acts with other men, and received in themselves the due penalty for their error.[29]

From this passage, we can see that God gave people over to shameful lusts.[29] It goes on to explain that those shameful lusts involved women exchanging what a natural sexual relationship is (woman with man) with an unnatural one (woman with woman).[29] It continues by telling us that men too "committed shameful acts with other men"[30]. We know what they are not God's desire for a relationship because he calls the acts "shameful". He also says that they, *"received in themselves the due penalty for their error."*[30]

This is not to say that God hates homosexuals. Scripture is simply saying that homosexuality is a sin and is not God's design for a marriage relationship. Like all sin, God calls us to turn away from sin and receive salvation through Christ's atonement. Liars are to turn from lying. Womanizers are to turn from womanizing, thieves are to stop stealing, fornicators are to cease from fornication and yes, homosexuality must be turned from as well.

Through faith in Christ which leads to repentance, salvation is equally offered to the liar, thief, fornicator and homosexual. In the next chapter we will study what it means to love. It's an important part of marriage.

COUPLE DISCUSSION QUESTIONS

Take some time to talk through the following questions. Allow equal time for both of you to talk and listen.

1) Read Romans chapter 1 together. What does it tell you about the relationship between a man and a woman?

2) What are some reasons polygamous relationships don't work?

3) How can additional people be involved in your marriage without it being polygamous marriage?

4) Read Genesis 16. How does another woman (Hagar) cause major problems for Abraham and Sarah? Did the fact that it was Sarah's idea make the relationship with Hagar any less destructive?

5) Tell your fiancé why he or she is the one person with whom you want to be married.

6) If there is something you or your spouse needs that you are unable to provide, how will you address it as a couple? Where will you turn for guidance and direction?

ENGAGEMENT

We would really be missing the boat if we didn't discuss the engagement period. The time between getting engaged and married is a time like no other, with its own struggles, stresses and temptations. It is in your best interest to discuss what you each expect as you approach the day of your wedding.

Men and women tend to look at the engagement period differently. After I got engaged, I wanted to get married as soon as possible. As a man, I figured, I'd already made the commitment by proposing. Let's get on with it. I had also saved myself sexually for my spouse. How much longer am I going to have to wait!

My bride-to-be saw engagement differently. Though I was ready to get married tomorrow, a short engagement was out of the question. She had dreamed of her wedding day since she was a fetus. Her mother had dreamed of her daughter's wedding day for even longer. And her father had dreaded that fateful day too long to allow some punk kid to deprive his daughter of the day she always dreamed of. It became apparent quite early that she had months of planning to do and it would be in my best interest to give her that time. For all of the grooms out there; listen closely. The wedding day is a big deal to your bride. She has expectations that give you an amazing opportunity to show her how much you love her. Your marriage will begin with a single day. Do all you can to make that day, as well as the days leading up to it, an indicator of the type of man you will be throughout your marriage.

All brides have different expectations from their grooms. Some brides want their groom to stay out of the planning altogether. Some grooms prefer to be left out of the planning, and for good reason. Guys tend to be a little less than excited about picking out dresses and flowers and dinner cutlery. We don't care what color doily matches the curtains at the reception hall. We just want to get married, have a fun reception and go on our honeymoon. That's why it is common for women to prepare for their weddings with their mother and friends.

When my wife was preparing for our wedding, I was reluctant to say too much because I wanted her wedding to be what SHE wanted. I was afraid that if I made suggestions, she may give me my way even though it wasn't what SHE wanted. Instead, I waited until my wife asked me for input and gave it to her when it was solicited.

The style and details of your wedding are yours to decide and will reflect who you are as a couple, however, there are a few suggestions I would like to make before we conclude. First, the length of your engagement shouldn't be too short or too long. Short engagements tend to cause unnecessary additional stress and limits your options in a number of areas. It will be hard to find the right wedding and reception venues on short notice. You may have difficulty booking the right wedding photographer, officiant, or caterer. Finding a wedding dress and getting it fitted takes time, as does the selection of bridesmaids' dresses and their fittings. Weddings involve coordinating a lot of people and that takes some time. Don't rush it.

On the other hand, it is not healthy to be engaged too long either. As a general rule, I believe eight to twelve months is a healthy engagement period. The engagement period is a time of limbo where you are committed to your future husband or wife, but not really committed officially. A couple can only last so long in that type of relationship. When a couple experiences too many life experiences in this type of limbo relationship, it will inevitably cause relationship problems. The vows you take at your wedding seal a commitment you promised to make when you got engaged. This commitment will get you through a lot of tough times. On the other hand, a commitment to make a commitment (engagement) doesn't have near the potency to hold you together during a time when the stress levels are high because a wedding is being planned.

> Just as you would seek the Lord in all you do as an individual, likewise seek Him in all you do as a couple. If He says, "Go left" go left. If He says, "Go right" go right. If He says, "Stay" then stay and if He says, "Go" then go. He is guiding you as a couple now. Follow Him together.

Second, unless you are doing a backyard wedding or going to Vegas, I suggest getting a wedding planner. You don't need the $6,000 wedding planner, just someone who has the wedding vendor relationships and can guide you through the process. When you buy a house, you use a real estate agent because the process of purchasing a home is complicated. Buying a home involves legal documents and escrow and title.

We use a professional to guide us through the process. Likewise, a wedding coordinator has the expertise and relationships to make what can be an extremely stressful process a lot more enjoyable.

Wedding planners can also save you money! Though you will have to pay the wedding planner, they may actually save you money due to the relationships they have with vendors such as photographers and D.Js. The wedding planner may know of venues that match your personality that you would have never found with your sophisticated "Google" search technique.

Wedding planners also reduce a lot of stress because you can leave the stress of planning to the planner. They know how many months before the wedding the venues should be booked. They know what the various items cost and can assure you that you are getting a good value for your money. In short, a wedding planner allows you to have your dream wedding and still enjoy the process of planning it. Isn't that what every bride wants?

Finally, I want to remind you that you aren't married yet. For some of you, sex has been a part of your relationship up until now. If that is the case, I would encourage you to abstain for now until you are married in anticipation of the wedding night. For others, you have been waiting for your wedding night to have sex and the temptation will increase as the big day approaches. It is easy to rationalize that because you know you will be getting married anyway, there will be no harm in having sex. I urge you to show self-control and see your commitment to abstinence through to your wedding night.

For those who have been married before, this is equally important. Living together and or having sex before you are married is clearly a sign that you want marriage on your own terms. You desire God's gift of marriage, but desire to change it to match your own desires. Are you not saying you know better than God? Consider taking God's gift of marriage as he designed and defined it so you can receive the joys and blessings of that gift rather than your own sinful version of it.

I wish you a blessed engagement and a marriage filled with love and joy. Marriage is a gift from God. Life is meant to be shared and I am happy God has led you to the one He has chosen with whom to share it.

The engagement period is the perfect time to begin establishing lifelong relational habits with one another. Do you pray together? Do you say, "I love you" as you get off the phone with each other? Do you attend a Bible study together? How do you bring up a heavy topic? How do you respond to tears by your fiancé? Now is the time to begin setting patterns for how you will do this as a married couple.

I leave you with a final admonishment. Just as you would seek the Lord in all you do as an individual, likewise seek Him in all you do as a couple. If He says, "Go left" go left. If He says, "Go right" go right. If He says, "Stay" then stay and if He says, "Go" then go. He is guiding you as a couple now. Follow Him together.

COUPLE DISCUSSION QUESTIONS

Take some time to talk through the following questions. Allow equal time for both of you to talk and listen.

1) What are your expectations regarding you and your fiancé's involvement in planning your wedding?

2) Given your situation as a couple, is a wedding planner a good idea?

3) Who will be involved in planning your wedding? Who will not?

4) If you could have everything you want in a wedding and reception, what would that look like?

5) If you have been living together, what is your plan moving forward? What do your decisions about living together and sex say about your view of God, His word, and your commitment to Him?

6) How will you keep yourselves from giving in to the temptation to have sex before your wedding day?

7) When things get stressful, how will you a handle it as a couple? How can your fiancé help you?

I Now Pronounce You . . .

Mark 10 says,

[7]'For this reason a man will leave his father and mother and be united to his wife, [8]and the two will become one flesh. 'So they are no longer two, but one flesh.

So, when and how does this transformation from single to married happen? What causes us to be married? The reason you've set a wedding date is ultimately for your status to change from single to married; to be transformed from two individuals to one flesh.

There are some who claim that being married in a church is necessary to make the marriage valid. Some have insisted that a pastor or priest must officiate for the marriage to be legitimate. Others may be a bit less dogmatic, claiming it is important to them, but not necessary for the marriage to be a true marriage in God's eyes.

There are differing views on the topic so I will share a few of them and then provide you with my own opinion. If this helps you with your dogmatic aunt who is insisting you must be married in a particular church by a particular type of minister, "You're Welcome."

> A man and wife become married upon pronouncement by someone speaking on behalf of God, whether it is a pastor, priest or government official.

One view is that a person is married at the moment they become one flesh through sexual intercourse. This could be interpreted a couple of ways. Some say that until a couple consummates their marriage sexually, they aren't really married, while others believe that the moment a couple comes together sexually they are married in the eyes of God.[44] From a Biblical perspective, neither of these seems consistent with the many incidents of sexual intercourse outside of marriage. It is inconsistent with Biblical passages such as the affair David had with Bathsheba or even the commandment not to commit adultery. If a person becomes married to every person they have sex with, there could be no sex outside of marriage since sex with that person immediately made them "Inside of marriage". For this reason, this view will not do.

Others say that you are married once you are legally married according to the government.[44] If you are in a place where either a judge or minister must officiate and a marriage license must be signed, then once those are accomplished, you are married. But this view has its pitfalls as well. Does this mean that Adam and Eve were never married because there was no government to legalize it?[44] Certainly not. We know Adam and Eve were married because in Genesis 3:6 Adam is called Eve's husband.[45]

Still, another view is that a marriage is valid in God's eyes when there is some type of ceremony. This view sees God bringing Eve to Adam in Genesis 2:22 comparable to the giving of a daughter away in a wedding ceremony.[44]

[22] *Then the Lord God made a woman from the rib he*

had taken out of the man, and he brought her to the man.

My own opinion goes back to our original understanding of marriage and of God. God is the creator of marriage as He is the creator of all things including the men and women who dwell upon His created earth. In Genesis 1, we see that God's method of creation is pronouncement. God speaks and things come into being. God speaks and light is separated from darkness. God speaks and two individuals become one.

Though there are no specific verses that say God pronounced Adam and Eve husband and wife, it seems probably that God told Adam that Eve was his wife. Without any prior precedent of what a wife was, how could he possibly know he had a wife without a verbal pronouncement of some type.

Therefore:

1) Because God places governments in positions of authority, valid marriage should comply with the legal requirements of the bride and groom in so far as these laws do not violate the commands of God.
2) A man and wife become married upon pronouncement by someone speaking on behalf of God, whether it is a pastor, priest, or government official.
3) There are no particularly sacred places that are required for a marriage to be valid in God's eyes unless they are given by God via governmental authority.

As a Christian standing at the altar proclaiming your vows in the presence of witnesses, realize that you are making sincere promises that not only God, but your friends and family will hear. With witnesses comes accountability not only to God and your spouse, but to the witnesses that heard you make a vow. Invited witnesses to your vow, have a right speak to you about your failure to keep it.

When you hear the pastor, priest or judge say, "I now pronounce you husband and wife." Know that the authority to make that pronouncement comes from God. He has given governments their authority and called pastors and priests to minister on His behalf. You enter a covenant that is bigger than your own promises. It is not created by your vows, but by God who created the institution of marriage itself.

COUPLE DISCUSSION QUESTIONS

Take time to talk through the following questions. Allow equal time for both of you to talk and listen.

1) Do you intend to be married in a church? Why or why is this not important to you?

2) Do you intend to be married by a pastor? Is this important to you and why?

3) Does it matter to you when you will be changed into one flesh? How do you interpret your union as a married couple coming to fruition?

4) How does God creating your unity as one flesh by pronouncement like he created heaven and earth by pronouncement affect your understanding of God's involvement in your marriage? Does God ever create that which is not good?

5) Read Genesis 2:22-23. What is the significance of God bringing the woman to Adam?

Marriage Roles

A women once told me she was excited to get married because she believed she would be married to her fiancé forever. Though the sentient was sweet, the statement was simply wrong. We aren't married to our spouse forever. We are married to them until we die physically on earth. That is why your vows say, "'til death do us part". Why does our marriage end when we die? Simply put, earthly marriage points us to heavenly marriage between Christ and the church. Once the church is united with Christ as the bride of Christ, there is no longer a need for marriage. We will already have the reality for which marriage pointed.

Our earthly marriage reflects a heavenly reality and by understanding the heavenly reality, we can better understand earthly marriage. More specifically, by understanding the love relationship between Christ and the church, we can better understand how husbands and wives are to love one another.

It is also important to recognize that earthly marriage and the marriage of Christ and the church are not equivalent. Men are not Christ and women are not the church, lest men decide to rule as if they are God. In no way are men deemed greater, more valuable, or wiser than women because men are identified with Christ in the Christ and church relationship. Though some men have tried to make such an argument, their argument is void the moment they fall short of the glory of God. Jesus' authority over the church is based on His divinity, not His masculinity. If, as a man, you are ever able to walk to your wife on water in omnipotence, omnipresence, holiness and divinity, perhaps then we can talk about you ruling over your wife. Until then, let's look at what Paul says in Ephesians 5:25-27:

[25] Husbands, love your wives, just as Christ loved the church and gave himself up for her [26] to make her holy, cleansing her by the washing with water through the word, [27] and to present her to himself as a radiant church, without stain or wrinkle or any other blemish, but holy and blameless. [16]

It is clear from this passage that a standard has been set for men, with regards to how they should treat their wives. Men are to love their wives as Christ loved the church. [17] How could anyone love another as Christ loved the church? Obviously, no one has love equal to that of God. Like the other standards of perfection set by God, this too is a mark that we should strive for, but will all fall short of. Romans 3:23 says, *"for all have sinned and fall short of the glory of God."*[48] But just because we fall short of God's glorious standard doesn't mean the standard is irrelevant. Men need to follow Christ's example as a husband.

In John 17, Jesus prays:

I pray for them. I am not praying for the world, but for those you have given me, for they are yours. [10]*all I have is yours, and all you have is mine. And glory has come to me through them.* [11]*I will remain in the world no longer, but they are still in the world, and I am coming to you. Holy father, protect them by the power of your name, the name you gave me, so that they may be one as we are one.* [12]*while I was with them, I protected them and kept them safe by that name you gave me. None has been lost except the one doomed to destruction so that scripture would be fulfilled.*[19]

Jesus is praying for His church (the bride of Christ). From Christ's example, we see that one of the husband's roles is to be a protector of his wife. Indeed, one of the greatest ways you can show your wife that you love her is to provide her with safety. Women want to feel secure and it is the responsibility of a husband to do what he can to provide that security.

Protection comes in many different forms. There is physical protection, emotional protection, financial stability and even relational stability. My wife is very careful to make sure the doors are locked on the cars and on the house. Sometimes, when we are tucked into bed, she will ask me if the front door is locked. By getting up out of bed and checking the front door, I provide her with an added sense of security.

I am not the type of person who goes around looking for a fight to pick, however, my wife knows that if faced with physical harm, I would do whatever necessary to physically protect her and my son. This is a Biblical concept.

[8] Jesus answered, "I told you that I am he. If you are looking for me, then let these men go." [9] this happened so that the words he had spoken would be fulfilled: "I have not lost one of those you gave me."[20]

John 10 says,

[11] "I am the good shepherd. The good shepherd lays down his life for the sheep. [12] The hired hand is not the shepherd and does not own the sheep. So when he sees the wolf coming, he abandons the sheep and runs away. Then the wolf attacks the flock and scatters it. [13] The man runs away because he is a hired hand and cares nothing for the sheep.

[14]"I am the good shepherd; I know my sheep and my sheep know me—[15]just as the Father knows me and I know the Father—and I lay down my life for the sheep.[21]"

Like a good husband, if danger comes to Christ's bride, He is willing to step into danger. He contrasts His actions with those of a hired hand who would run away, caring more about his own safety than that of the sheep. Jesus sacrifices himself for His spouse. Husbands need to be men of honor, willing to sacrifice themselves for their wives. Men want to be respected by their wives, but respect is something to be earned. It will be hard for a woman to respect a man who is unwilling to protect her in the face of danger.

This protection is more than merely physical. Women need to feel secure emotionally as well. If a man is constantly telling his wife that he wants to leave her every time they have an argument, a women will feel the insecurity of the relationship. Again, we turn to scripture, this time seeing God's relationship with His people Israel.

No one will be able to stand against you all the days of your life. As I was with Moses, so I will be with you; I will never leave you nor forsake you.[22]

We all make this vow to each other when we get married. The difference is that when God says He won't leave His people, He follows through. If we were unable to take God at His word when He makes this promise, the people of God would live in uncertainty. We need the security of knowing that God will not leave us, regardless of what we may do or say. Likewise, wives need to know that their husbands are not going anywhere. Husbands should be able to say to their wives, "I will never leave you nor forsake you."[22]

Men should be providers for their wives as well. This doesn't mean that a husband must pour riches upon his wife, but rather that He should provide for his family's needs. It doesn't even mean that a wife can't work or even make more money than her husband, but, scripture is filled with numerous passages where God is our provider and the people find their security in God taking care of them. In the Old Testament God provided for His people in the desert by giving them quail and manna to eat. Exodus 16 says:

That evening quail came and covered the camp, and in the morning there was a layer of dew around the camp. [14] When the dew was gone, thin flakes like frost on the ground appeared on the desert floor.[23]

In the New Testament, Jesus provides wine at a wedding[24], healing to the sick, and bread and fish to the five thousand.[25] Jesus provides for His bride. Husbands must do the same.

If we look at the church, we see people with wonderful gifts, accomplishing great things for God. We see the bride of Christ actively working and striving to minister as Christ works in and through them to empower and guide. Likewise, women should feel the freedom to actively work and strive to accomplish great things knowing they have a husband by their side ready to help empower and guide them.

Roles are important, however. The roles of men and women are distinct, yet both require submission. Submission, in this case, is an action and attitude. It is not forced upon you, but rather, is a personal act of your will. Jesus submitted to the Father. He made a conscious decision to position Himself lower than God the Father and to be about His Father's will. The greatness of Christ is found in the way He accomplished everything from healing the sick to raising the dead to saving men from their sins. He did it all by submission rather than authoritative might.

Ephesians 5:21-33 says,

[21] Submit yourselves to one another because of your reverence for Christ.

[22] Wives, submit yourselves to your husbands as to the Lord. [23] For a husband has authority over his wife just as Christ has authority over the church; and Christ is himself the Savior of the church, his body. [24] And so wives must submit themselves completely to their husbands just as the church submits itself to Christ.

25 Husbands, love your wives just as Christ loved the church and gave his life for it. 26 He did this to dedicate the church to God by his word, after making it clean by washing it in water, 27 in order to present the church to himself in all its beauty—pure and faultless, without spot or wrinkle or any other imperfection. 28 Men ought to love their wives just as they love their own bodies. A man who loves his wife loves himself. (29 None of us ever hate our own bodies. Instead, we feed them, and take care of them, just as Christ does the church; 30 for we are members of his body.) 31 As the scripture says, "For this reason a man will leave his father and mother and unite with his wife, and the two will become one." 32 There is a deep secret truth revealed in this scripture, which I understand as applying to Christ and the church. 33 But it also applies to you: every husband must love his wife as himself, and every wife must respect her husband.

In our relationships with God, we are not forced to submit to God. Instead, we come to a place where we agree with God even if we don't completely understand His reasoning. We may not always see eye to eye, but when push comes to shove, the correct response will be to follow God's lead. In marriage this is illustrated by the roles of the husband and the wife.

In all relationships, whether marital, personal, business or church, order requires that someone have the final say. Good managers and business owners will seek what is best not only for themselves, but for their employees, shareholders, and customers. Good pastors and church boards will seek to follow the Lord's leading. Ultimately, however, the CEO, manager, Pastor or Board must make the final decision and the rest of the corporation must submit to that decision. If the decision was wrong, the responsibility will fall on the one who made the final decision.

> The greatness of Christ is found in the way He accomplished everything from healing the sick to raising the dead to saving men from their sins. He did it all by submission rather than authoritative might.

In the Ephesians passage, God directs both the husband and the wife to submit to each other out of reverence for the Lord (vs 21). As a couple we are not lording over each other but serving one another. Authority, however, is granted to the husband in verses 22 and 23. When the final decision is made, the responsibility before God falls upon the husband, because God has given him the authority. With the authority comes the responsibility.

Finally, in 1 John 4:19 it says, "*We love because he first loved us.*"[26]

It is because of the love we receive *from* Jesus that we love Him in return. For the soon to be husband or the newly married, this truth should be your mantra. Love her first. Show her you love her by your deeds. Protect her and provide for her and see if this doesn't cause her to love and respect you.

Ultimately, as a couple, we depend upon God to provide for our needs. Security in the family is found in trusting the Lord with our future. It's important that wives see their husbands take the role of provider and protector seriously, but it is as important that she sees her husband's dependance upon God for the family's protection and provision.

COUPLE DISCUSSION QUESTIONS

Take some time to talk through the following questions. Allow equal time for both of you to talk and listen.

1) As a husband, are you prepared to be a protector and provider of your wife?

2) As a wife, what are your expectations for your husband regarding your security? What do you want him to do and say?

3) How can a husband best show his wife that he will never leave her or forsake her?

4) If your husband does everything he can to protect and provide for you, how will that cause you to respond? How will that make you feel?

5) What can you do as a couple to keep each other focused on God as your ultimate protector and provider?

6) Talk about how you see your role in your marriage with regards to submission, authority, love?

7) How will you make major decisions as a couple?

CHOOSING TO LOVE – PART 1

One of the most popular passages of scripture read at weddings is 1 Corinthians chapter 13 regarding love. If you've ever been to a wedding, you probably heard it. I find it rather humorous that the passage is usually read in its entirety which includes discussion about tongues and prophecy. Tongues and prophecy generally don't have anything to do with a wedding covenant, unless you are Pentecostal, and someone prophesied that you were to marry your fiancé.

What may surprise some of you is that the passage in 1 Corinthians 13 is not written about marriage. In context, the passage is discussing spiritual gifts and how gifts from God are as useless as a clanging gong when they aren't bed-rocked in love for others. For example, what good is it to speak in an unknown tongue in a church service if no one in the service can understand it and be helped by the word. Gifts are useless without love and as we said from the beginning, "Marriage is not only one of the greatest gifts God gives us, but it is one of the first gifts given to man." Therefore, let's learn more about how to love from this famous passage.

1 Corinthians 13:4-13 says,

Love is patient, love is kind. It does not envy, it does not boast, it is not proud. [5] It does not dishonor others, it is not self-seeking, it is not easily angered, it keeps no record of wrongs. [6] Love does not delight in evil but rejoices with the truth. [7] It always protects, always trusts, always hopes, always perseveres. [8] Love never fails. But where there are prophecies, they will cease; where there are tongues, they will be stilled; where there is knowledge, it will pass away. [9] For we know in part and we prophesy in part, [10] but when completeness comes, what is in part disappears. [11] When I was a child, I talked like a child, I thought like a child, I reasoned like a child. When I became a man, I put the ways of childhood behind me. [12] For now we see only a reflection as in a mirror; then we shall see face to face. Now I know in part; then I shall know fully, even as I am fully known [13] And now these three remain: faith, hope and love. But the greatest of these is love.[31]

The reason many couples read verse 8-12 is because

they like verse 13. This verse says that love is greater than faith and hope. The meat of the passage, however, is in verse 4-7. In these verses, we see a number of words used to help us understand what love is.

We often hear people describe love as something they fell into, as if by accident, they tripped and stepped in something. They portray love as a feeling on par with hate, tiredness or indigestion. But, through scripture, God gives us the truth about love. Love is a choice. Love is action. We love someone by what we do and not by how we feel.

When I was an undergraduate student at Wheaton College, I remember being distressed because I didn't think I loved God. I went to Don Church, my college cross country coach and explained to him that I didn't think I loved God. He asked, "What makes you think you don't love God?" I replied, "I've been in love before, and I don't feel that way about God." His reply still echoes in my mind, "You don't know that you love God by how you feel. You know that you love God by what you do." Jesus said, "If you love me, you will obey what I command."[32]

One of the primary arguments people give for divorcing their spouse is that they no longer love that person. Mistakenly, many approach love as a feeling on which marriage and actions depend. If you view marriage this way, you are doomed to fail because I can almost guarantee your feelings of love will come and go. Successful marriages are built on commitment to love someone even when we aren't feelin' it.

Feelings often follow actions. Speaking about money, Jesus said in Matthew 6:21, "For where your treasure is, there your heart will be also." The point is that your heart will care for what you invest in. If you invest your time, money and devotion in your spouse, your heart will follow.

Indeed, love is all about what you do. In marriage, feelings will come and go, but love will remain forever, if you choose to love each other. Verse 4 says, *"Love is patient, love is kind. It does not envy, it does not boast, it is not proud."*[33] This list of love's attributes is also a list of the attributes of God, for according to scripture, God is love.[34] Love is patient. What this means is that when we are patient, we are expressing an attribute of love. Love is kind. When you are kind to someone, you are expressing an attribute of love.

In practical terms, this means that to love our spouse, we must choose to put these attributes of love into action. I dare say that the degree to which you love someone is related to the degree in which you choose to exemplify the attributes of love. For instance, you are going out to dinner with another couple and your wife is taking a long, long, long, long time. Trust me men. If this hasn't happened to you yet, it will. Your natural tendency will be to get bent out of shape and throw away your watch in exchange for a calendar just to show her how long she is taking. That is not love. Love is patient. When given the choice to get frustrated and impatient or to be loving by demonstrating patience, we must choose to love. We choose love not only because we vowed to love our spouse, but because choosing to love is choosing to be more like God and bearing his image is our primary role as a human being.

Love doesn't envy. To envy is to desire to have or be something another has. We are not to feel this way toward our spouse or anyone else. To envy is to deny love because envy focuses on self rather than the other person.

Love doesn't boast. A good spouse doesn't need to boast. As Paul says in Corinthians, "Let him who boasts boast in the Lord".[35] Boasting is a means of building yourself up in the eyes of someone else. If a man boasts about how much money he makes or how important he is, he is ultimately seeking his own gain over those of his partner. His motive for boasting is to get the other person to think higher of him. This is not love, but selfishness.

In the same way, love isn't proud. Pride is the sin that caused Satan to rebel against God.[36] Pride is ultimately a lie. We lie to ourselves convincing ourselves that we are more than we are. When we think we are more than we are, we fail to love, fail to be honest and fail to be content, with what we have been given (including our spouse). Imagine believing you deserve better than the spouse God graciously gave you. To believe that way is to disagree with God, yet many use this as an excuse to leave a marriage.

Love isn't rude. This is a tough one for guys, but I've met a gal or two who could compete with the big boys in this category. I believe rudeness shows up in relationships for a couple of reasons. The longer you are married, the less concerned we become about being on our best behavior. For instance, you would have never passed gas on your first date, but now that you've been married ten years, the desire to be discreet has lost its appeal. "She will love me anyway", we rationalize. True as this may be, choosing to be rude is choosing to not love your spouse. You are making a decision to do something your spouse will not like simply because you can. That's not love. Some, however, are rude because they are insecure in their relationship. The statement, "she will love me anyway", becomes a question, "Will she love me anyway?" Marriage is not a pop quiz. If it were, the person who chose to be rude would fail miserably.

Love isn't self-seeking. Imagine what your marriage would be like if as a husband, you committed to always do what was best for your wife. And imagine that as a wife, you were always seeking the best for your husband. This is how marriage is meant to work. Your responsibility as a spouse is to seek the best for your spouse above your own interests. You shouldn't need to seek after your own best interests because that's your spouse's job.

The fact that love is not easily angered is a rather relative statement in that the term "easily" is subjective. For the sake of practicality, think of it this way. It takes a lot for a loving person to get angry. If you find yourself getting angry at the drop of a hat, this is not love. Love keeps a person from striking out in anger. Trust me. Your spouse is going to push your buttons. From time to time, you are going to get angry, but genuine love is what keeps the anger embers at bay.

> Imagine believing you deserve better than the spouse God graciously gave you. To believe that way is to disagree with God, yet many use this as an excuse to leave a marriage.

Quite possibly, the most relevant for the married couple is the admonition that love doesn't keep a score of wrongs. Healthy relationships require the ability to come before your partner with a clean slate. Nobody wants to be in a relationship where they are always trying to make up for their mistakes. This concept is beautifully modeled by God in the way He forgives us. Once God forgives you of your sins, He never brings it up again. A healthy marriage requires that the score card be thrown out. When your spouse hurts you, forgive them and never bring it up again. What your spouse did to hurt you may well be damaging to your marriage, but once you have forgiven, holding on to that wrong as ammunition for the future is equally as damaging. Let it go.

We've covered some very important aspects of love, which are necessary for a successful marriage. In our next chapter, we will continue learning ways to love our spouse.

COUPLE DISCUSSION QUESTIONS

Take some time to talk through the following questions. Allow equal time for both of you to talk and listen.

1) Based on what we learned in this chapter, tell your fiancé what it means that you love them.

2) In what ways does your spouse try your patience?

3) In what ways has your spouse shown rudeness? How have you been rude to your spouse? Can you commit to change this for the sake of love for your spouse?

4) Love isn't self-seeking. Tell your spouse how they can better seek what is best for you.

5) What makes you angry? Talk through ways you can avoid expressing anger.

6) Do you believe that you are marrying the person God believes is best for you? If this person is best for you, would it be fair to say that if thinking someone or something else is better would be a lie both now and tomorrow?

CHOOSING TO LOVE- PART 2

In the last chapter, we looked at most of "the love chapter" in 1 Corinthians 13. In this chapter we will continue to glean marital wisdom from the verses that remain. Verse 6 tells us that *"Love does not delight in evil but rejoices with the truth".[37]* Note that God is showing us that "delighting in evil" is antithetical to "rejoicing with the truth". He uses the word "delight" to describe the feeling toward evil, but the word "rejoice" in reference to truth.

When we choose to love, we choose to find joy in being truthful. We find joy in knowing that we are not living a lie. We are transparent and honest. There is great joy in that kind of living and it is the way our relationships should be when we choose to love someone.

The antithesis of this characteristic of love is to "delight in evil". Evil comes in thousands of grotesque shapes and sizes. When we choose to enjoy evil thoughts and deeds, we are not loving. Take note that the passage doesn't specify who the doer of evil is. Perhaps the reason is that it doesn't matter. If you love someone, you won't delight in their evil deeds, nor will you delight in your own.

Verse 7 tells us that *"It always protects, always trusts, always hopes, always perseveres."*[38] This is one of the most relevant passages for married couples today. Let's look at the first two statements together and then the last two statements.

Married individuals must protect their partners. This isn't just physical protection, but emotional, spiritual, and psychological as well. One way that men may lovingly express this principle is by showing their wife or fiancé they are protected. When a spider is found in the shower, rush up and save the day. When a stranger knocks on the door, don't let her get up to answer it, but as the protector, get up and see who it is. By doing so, you are showing that she is protected, and she will feel loved.

Men are not as vulnerable physically, as we are emotionally and psychologically. When your husband comes home with a beat up ego from being devalued at work through words and actions, a good wife can show her love by protecting him emotionally and psychologically. There have been many afternoons and evenings when I have come home feeling worthless as a pastor and a man. Fortunately, my wife was quick to protect my emotional and psychological well-being by building me up. Better yet, she did this by telling me the truth about me. She didn't feed me a bunch of bologna just to make me feel better, but instead, filled me with the truth about my abilities, character, and actions. Every man needs a good wife to protect his ego and every woman needs a good man to protect her physically.

> Love is about choices. Every day, you have an opportunity to choose to love your fiancé or spouse. You have an opportunity to choose to hope and persevere.

We both need to protect each other spiritually. One way I love my wife is to protect her in this area of her life. If my wife begins to speak or act in a way that is unrighteous, I can protect her by calling her attention to the truth about these actions. Likewise, if my wife sees me straying spiritually, it is her loving duty to protect me by bringing it to my attention.

I accept this protection because I trust my wife. Protection and trust are related. To truly be safe in the protection of another, we must trust them enough to submit to the authority of their protection.

Imagine for a moment that the police commissioned to protect us were not trusted by any of the citizens of the town they were charged to protect. When a house was robbed, the police wouldn't get called because they weren't trusted. As a husband and wife, the husband must put his trust in his wife and vice-versa. Again, we must actively choose to trust and actively choose to protect.

Finally, the passage says that love "always hopes" and "always perseveres".[39] Again, these two verses go together. Hope is a powerful thing and without it, we could never persevere. Though the saying goes that life will throw you the occasional curveball, I've found that life sometimes intentionally beams you in the head. It drops you to the ground demanding you decide whether to get back in the batter's box. It is hope that you might get a hit or better yet, hit a homerun that motivates you to dust yourself off and persevere by stepping back into the box.

In marriage, perseverance is becoming less and less common. After getting beamed in the head a few times, many couples decide to call it quits. "Why would

I risk getting beamed in the head again?" See if some of these baseball analogies ring familiar to the reasons many couples don't persevere.

"I'm just not cut out for this sport." "My style doesn't fit this team." "This team doesn't have the potential to go all the way!" "This other team has offered me more." "This city doesn't appreciate me."

But God says that love perseveres. Love doesn't give up. To persevere, however, we must have hope. For this reason, it is important for couples to dream together and set plans together. It's why couples should endeavor to conquer new challenges and rejoice in goals they've reached. It's the reason it's important for couples to make long term goals together and work side by side to accomplish those goals. We persevere in the hard times because we have hope for what is to come.

Love is about choices. Every day, you have an opportunity to choose to love your fiancé or spouse. You have an opportunity to choose to hope and persevere. When all the dust settles from life, you will find there will be those who, when faced with adversity and trouble in their marriage, found hope and chose to persevere and those who, when faced with adversity and trouble in their marriage, instead chose to call it quits. My prayer is that when life's fastball drops you to the ground, you find hope in your spouse, in your marriage and the God who created them both. I hope you choose to step back into the batter's box over and over and over again.

COUPLE DISCUSSION QUESTIONS

Take a few minutes to talk through the following questions. Allow equal time for both of you to talk and listen.

1) In what ways do you feel you are most in need of protection from your fiancé or spouse?

2) Do you trust your spouse? What could your spouse do to cause you to trust him/her more?

3) What are some of your hopes and dreams regarding your spouse and your marriage?

4) Where do you see yourselves in 20 years?

5) When life throws you a fastball at the head and drops you to the ground, what will motivate you to keep going?

6) Why will your marriage last when others don't?

7) Have you been truthful with each other? Is there anything you have not been truthful about that you need to bring to light?

MARRIAGE KILLER #1
FAILING WITH MONEY

In my pastoral career, I have found that there are primarily three things you need to watch out for that can potentially kill your marriage. One is the way you communicate with each other. If you don't communicate right, it can kill your marriage. Another marriage killer is infidelity. Having sex with someone other than your spouse can kill your marriage.

O.k.! Let me stop for a second. You're saying, "Thanks for the tip there, Captain Obvious! Of course having sex with someone other than your spouse can kill your marriage!" I'm stating it, however, because thousands of marriages are left in shambles every year because people have sex outside of the marriage covenant. Some of you reading this are couples who are not married, but have been having sex outside of the marriage covenant. For some reason, folks aren't getting the picture.

The third marriage killer is money and will be the focus of this chapter. It has been suggested to me that children should be added to this list of marriage killers, especially when dealing with a second marriage and the children are from previous marriages. I, however, believe that if you manage money, communication, and sex as a couple in an effective way, children will less likely be a potent marriage killer.

Money related problems can cause serious marriage problems because money tends to be what individuals see as their lifeline. When we don't have enough money, we get worried and look for a way to solve the problem. Unfortunately, many couples look for someone to blame first. If you don't want to take responsibility for your financial problems, there's only one other person in your marriage for you to point the finger. For most men, it is difficult when they are having trouble providing for their family. Men have an internal need to be a breadwinner and provider. When a man is struggling to provide, he may feel less of a man.

It is not only for the family needs that a man wants to provide. He wants to provide for his family's wants as well. Unfortunately, if a couple does not have a financial plan, an individual's wants can break a couple financially. Though a man may bring in a good salary, he can feel like he is failing if he or his wife is spending more money than he can make.

Though money can be a marriage killer, money itself is not the ultimate problem. Mismanagement is. Money problems bring up different fears and frustrations for the husband and the wife. The wife may feel she is not being cared for, listened too, provided for, or loved enough. A man may feel that his wife does not respect his financial plan for the family and as a result feels disrespected. If a woman doesn't feel loved or cared for and a man doesn't feel respected as a provider, your marriage will be in trouble.

The best way to immune yourselves from the marriage killer of money is to get on the same page financially from the very beginning and communicate regularly about your financial plans as a couple. There's a couple I am very close with who was considering marriage. However, the woman was accepted to graduate school before they could get engaged. I encouraged them that if they were going to get engaged, they needed to see her school debt as "their" debt and not just hers. They got engaged looking to the future together.

Couples need to approach finances as a team and plan and communicate as a team. I was counseling with a couple a few years ago that had separated their bills so the husband paid certain bills and the wife paid other bills. They had divided the financial responsibilities. They each earned their own money and had their own bank accounts. They are now divorced. Do you know why? Because trying to be one and divided at the same time is stupid. This couple's way of handling finances was a marriage killer from the start! When you get married, it belongs to you both. Along these same lines, if you are planning to get married and have a pre-nuptial agreement, do yourself a favor and not get married. By planning for what you will do "if" you get divorced, you are planning to fail. You are also keeping yourself from being one with your spouse before you ever enter the marriage covenant.

> The best way to immune yourselves from the marriage killer of money is to get on the same page financially from the very beginning and communicate regularly about your financial plans as a couple.

Before you go any farther, you need to get on the same page financially. You need to plan TOGETHER. Planning together financially is called a budget and this is how it works. Get out a piece of paper or put together an Excel spreadsheet or whatever gets the job done. Start by listing all your projected income. If you make $30,000 a year, divide $30,000 by 12 months and you will have your monthly income. If you both work, add the two incomes together and divide by twelve months. As a couple, you need to know how much money you make together.

Next, you need to plan for how much money you will spend in a month. List your rent, utilities, car payment, and anything else for which you will be spending money. Decide how much money you will each have to spend on "whatever". Your "whatever" money might be for a daily latte or a pair of shoes at the mall. The point is that you need to determine together how much money will be spent in the next month before the next month happens. Agree as a couple that you will control your money, rather than having individual financial decisions by one spouse or the other control your marriage. Trust me on this. If each of you go out into the world and just spend money without an agreed upon plan, your marriage will suffer. Create a budget together and stick with it. Don't spend a dime as a married couple until you've communicated with each other and determined how you as a couple will spend that money.

Money can cause problems whether you don't have enough of it or have plenty. That's because money is never the real problem. Money simply provides a catalyst for other issues to work their way out.

When couples are struggling to pay the bills there can

be a lot of stress. They become desperate and search for any way to relieve the pressure. When couples have plenty of money, they can easily get lost in the love of what money can provide for them individually. Both problems stem from a lack of dependance upon God.

To avoid the marriage killer of failure with money you must, as a couple, find your security and provision in God. If you are struggling financially and God is not the one you depend on, you will in desperation do things damaging to your relationship with God and your marriage. If you are blessed financially, don't allow the pleasures that it provides to take priority over your relationship with God and your spouse.

BUDGET EXERCISE

Take some time as a couple and put together a budget to which you both agree.

Tithe $_____

House Payment/Rent $_____

Car Payment $_____

Utility Bills $_____

Phone Bill $_____

Payment on debt $_____

Husband spending money $_____

Wife spending money $_____

Student Loan Payment $_____

Health Insurance $_____

Investments $_____

Car insurance $_____

Total Expenses $_____(Minus) Total Income$ _____

Balance $_____

COUPLE DISCUSSION QUESTIONS

Take time to talk through the following questions. Allow equal time for both of you to talk and listen.

1) Do you consider yourself to be responsible with money?

2) What kind of debt are you bringing into this marriage and how do you intend to handle that debt together? What concerns do you have?

3) Who will most likely be the person to pay the bills, balance the checkbook, etc.

4) What is your plan for tithing? Retirement planning? Children's college fund? Paying down debt? Saving for a home?

5) What dreams do you have for the future that will have a significant impact on your finances?

6) Do you intend to have any separate accounts that are not available to your spouse? If so, why? What does this say about your trust for one another and oneness as a couple?

7) What are your personal financial ambitions? To be wealthy? To be comfortable? To be happy? To be secure? What does that mean to each of you?

MARRIAGE KILLER #2
FAILING TO COMMUNICATE

All relationships involve some type of communication. You will find that the closer a relationship is, the more we drop our guard with respect to communication. The reason is simple. When we believe we will be loved regardless of what we say, we tend to be less concerned about what we say.

The more comfortable you get in a relationship, the less hiding and pretending we tend to do. As a new couple, you may go to the bathroom with the door shut and locked and then spray deodorizer before you leave. After twenty years, you may not even close the door anymore. A married man may walk around the house at ten o'clock at night in his underwear, but if someone rings the doorbell, he's gonna throw on some sweats and a t-shirt.

Likewise, we tend to allow hurtful things to come out of our mouths to people we love that we would never say to a neighbor or our boss. What we say and do are all ways that we communicate. If I show more respect to my boss than I show my spouse, I am communicating something. If I am kinder to my neighbor than I am my spouse, I am communicating something. And if I appear to want to spend more time at work than with my spouse, I am communicating something.

> If I don't speak to her in a manner that says she is the most important woman on earth to me, I am communicating to her that others are more important. If I don't speak to her with the consistency due a person I share my entire life with, I am communicating that sharing my entire life with her is not what I want.

Words are powerful, but so is silence. I remember being upset with my wife one day early in our marriage. Rather than talk it out, I went and took a nap for a few hours. When I woke, she was crying. By not talking about it, I made it worse. The absence of clarifying communication invited her to speculate as to why I might be upset and that speculation only caused insecurity and hurt. There have been other times when stress has gotten the best of me. Many times, when I am under a great amount of stress, I will get very quiet as I try to figure things out. Sometimes, my wife will think I am upset with her because I am not speaking with her. She thinks there is a relationship problem, when the reality is I have a stress problem.

At the core of this lesson is this. Couples must stay in continual communication in a manner consistent with their intimacy level. When I talk to my wife, I must talk to her like she is the most important woman on the face of the earth. I must speak to her like she is the mother of my son. I must talk to her with the consistency due a person I share my entire life. When we speak, I must speak to her the way I would speak to someone I love. The reason is simple. If I don't do this, I am actually communicating something I don't want to communicate to my wife.

If I don't speak to her in a manner that says she is the most important woman on earth to me, I am communicating to her that others are more important. If I don't speak to her with the consistency due a person I share my entire life with, I am communicating that sharing my entire life with her is not what I want.

It is easy to see how poor communication can kill a marriage. We all tend to say stupid things sometimes.

We all sometimes neglect saying those things we know we should say. Over time, feelings change, life happens, and communication may fall to the bottom of your list of priorities. Don't allow yourself to take each other for granted. Never assume you can say whatever you want to your spouse and get away with it. You are not immune from consequences because you had a bad day and spouted off to your spouse. Words can hurt and kill marriages.

Because life is busy, it is important to set aside time to communicate. Put it on your calendar. A wonderful habit for couples to get into is date night. Pick a day or night of the week and spend time alone together. You can go out to dinner or see a movie, but have some time during your date when you can simply open up and talk about life. Share your dreams, fears, struggles and hopes. As you have children, drop the kids off at grandma's and continue this habit. It is vital to your marriage. By simply setting the time aside, we communicate to each other how important our relationship is.

Communication is one of the ways we share with our spouse who we are and what we care about. It's the way we allow our spouse to share in our weakness so that they understand to whom they are married. We build trust in one another by observing how our spouse responds to our struggles and failures. Before my wife and I married, I was very honest with her about my many shortcomings. She learned of my struggles and frustrations, and I learned of hers. Because they were clearly communicated, she can help me through my struggles, and I can help her through hers. When I fail, it is not a big letdown to her because she knows who she married. Failing to communicate the real you before getting married can leave your spouse feeling victim to the old bait and switch. "I thought I married this person, but now I know different."

Lay who you are out on the table today. Express your real hopes and dreams and shortfalls. Make a commitment to continually communicate in a manner consistent with your intimacy level. Remember that silence is a form of communication. Communicate regularly and lovingly and you will immune yourself from this marriage killer.

COUPLE DISCUSSION QUESTIONS

Take some time to talk through the following questions. Allow equal time for both of you to talk and listen.

1) What are some areas you have not communicated about that are important to you?

2) When you have something that is important for you to talk about, what would be the worse way for your spouse to respond?

3) What do you need from your spouse to enable clear communication?

4) When is communication most difficult for you? (example: right after work, late at night) How can you deal with this as a couple to keep communication clear?

5) Is there anything in your past or family upbringing that could affect your ability to communicate well with your spouse?

6) What is it and how will you overcome it?

7) How can you get the attention of your spouse so he/she knows that you have something important to communicate?

MARRIAGE KILLER #3
FAILING SEXUALLY

If you can't figure this one out, you should probably just stay single. To put it bluntly, sex with anyone other than your spouse can kill your marriage. Now some of you will want to play Bill Clinton and debate what the meaning of the word, "is" is. What is sex? If you want to play that game, don't get married. Your spouse deserves your faithfulness when it comes to intimacy both physically and emotionally.

Couples come to the issue of sex with their own individual pasts and experiences. Some were raised in homes where promiscuity was common or where there weren't two parents to be faithful to one another. It is not uncommon to have children grow up with only a mom around who had numerous boyfriends or husbands rotating through the house. These experiences can taint the way we see the marriage relationship, making it important to get our view of marriage from God rather than our own experience.

The Garden of Eden paints a wonderful picture of the marriage relationship. Adam is given Eve as his wife and told, "Be fruitful and increase in number; fill the earth and subdue it."[40] In other words, God tells them to have sex. It's not only okay for them to have sex, but it's part of God's plan for them. Recognize however, that He is speaking to them as a couple and not individually. Notice also, that there are no other women for Adam to have sex with. Let me say that again in case you missed it. THERE ARE NO OTHER WOMEN FOR ADAM TO HAVE SEX WITH! Yes, it's true, there weren't any other women on the earth, and that's the point. God created Eve to be the perfect helper for Adam. When God gives you a wife, THERE ARE NO OTHER WOMEN TO HAVE SEX WITH.

For you women, notice that Eve was created for Adam. She wasn't created to be the wife or sexual partner of anyone else. THERE ARE NO OTHER MEN ON EARTH TO HAVE SEX WITH. There were no swinger parties in the garden. The garden is the model of a marriage done right sexually.

As you go through marriage, you will notice other men and women. My wife isn't the only beautiful woman on earth, though she is very beautiful! But in the marriage garden that God has given my wife and I, THERE ARE NO OTHER WOMEN TO HAVE SEX WITH. If I look around this garden called my marriage, there are only two people; Julie and I.

You may argue it is absurd to compare the garden to the way the world is now. After all, there was no variety in the garden like there is today. Adam didn't have a choice to have sex with anyone other than Eve. She was the only other human being on earth. True. But I'm not talking about who is on the earth. I'm talking about marriage and comparing the marriage covenant to the garden. And in your marriage garden, THERE IS NO OTHER PERSON TO HAVE SEX WITH.

You may recall a few years ago there was quite a stir about speculation that Jesus had been married to Mary Magdalene. It erupted primarily as a result of the book by Dan Brown called "The Di Vinci Code" which claimed Jesus and Mary had been married and conceived a child.[41] In my reading of scripture however, Jesus seems to already have a bride and that bride is the church. Jesus isn't married to both the church and Mary Magdalene. He isn't a polygamist!

The example of Christ is of a faithful husband who Ephesians 5:25-27 says,

Husbands, love your wives, just as Christ loved the church and gave himself up for her [26] *to make her holy, cleansing her by the washing with water through the*

word, [27]and to present her to himself as a radiant church, without stain or wrinkle or any other blemish, but holy and blameless.[42]

It seems clear that Jesus cares about the purity of his bride, the church. He went to incredible measures to secure her purity.

Sex is more than a physical act and we all know it. We care not only about sexual faithfulness, but emotional faithfulness as well. Quite practically, the way you relate to people of the opposite sex must change when you get married. What was innocent flirting before you got engaged is an offense to your spouse now. What was a playful look before, can be hurtful now. We feel threatened when we sense a third person invading our garden, and rightfully so.

The reason any of this is an issue is because both men and women have sexual desires. Marriage is the place where those desires are rightfully fulfilled. When one spouse doesn't have a desire for sexual intimacy, the desire does not necessarily go away for the other and this is where temptation can get the better of a person. Fortunately, God understands this and addresses this issue in his word.

1 Corinthians 7:4 says,

Do not deprive each other except perhaps by mutual consent and for a time, so that you may devote yourselves to prayer. Then come together again so that

Satan will not tempt you because of your lack of self-control.

As a married couple you are one flesh and should care about the desires of your spouse and how to help him or her manage sexual temptation. It's important to be forthcoming about when you are desiring sex. Sometimes you will have sex when you don't have the desire, but when your spouse needs it to keep his/her desires under control. Many men and women have gone outside of the marriage to fulfill sexual desires because they weren't being met within the marriage. Work together to keep each other victorious in marital and sexual purity.

Take some time to talk about sex. It's going to be a part of your life from your wedding night on. Discuss your fears and insecurities. Be open about your expectations being clear about what is "not okay." For some, past indiscretions with sex should be shared so there will be no surprises down the road. It's important to know who's in your garden.

COUPLE DISCUSSION QUESTIONS

Spend a bit of time talking through the following questions. Allow equal time for both of you to talk and listen.

1) What was the example of your mother and/or father regarding promiscuity and sexual fidelity?

2) What has your own personal experience been? How might this shape your attitude moving forward?

3) What are your expectations of yourself and of your fiancé in this area?

4) Communicate clearly what you believe you would do if you found your fiancé to be unfaithful to you.

5) Are you in this together with regards to meeting each other's sexual needs?

6) As you grow past the honeymoon phase, if one of you desires to have sex more often than the other, how will you handle that? How will you help your spouse avoid sexual temptation?

7) Look each other in the eye and make a commitment to each other that you will be faithful to one another.

PARENTING AS A COUPLE

One of the blessings we often anticipate as a married couple is the possibility of one day having children. Sometimes, couples are only married a month and find out they are pregnant, while other couples may take years to conceive. Still others choose not to have children or are unable to conceive.

My wife and I decided to wait a few years to have children so that we could simply enjoy being married for a while. We used birth control for about three years until we decided we would like to have a child. For us, however, having a child was not as simple as getting off the pill. After about eight years of marriage, it began to look as though God didn't want us to have children. We would be content with God's plan and prepare for a child-free life. Since we weren't going to be having any children, I figured I was going to be saving a lot of money. After all, children are expensive. So, I started a rather major remodel on our bathroom. Wouldn't you know, about the time we determined we wouldn't be having a child, my wife woke me up one morning with a freshly peed-on stick announcing we were having a baby. My life changed forever.

> Children need to know they are the priority of both parents together, not of each parent separately. A child should never have to be confronted with the question of who loves them more, mom or dad. They are a unit that loves one another, and that love has brought the child into the world to be loved by them both . . . together.

Kids don't change everything, but almost. I'm so happy to have had those years with my wife before we conceived, yet I treasure every day I have with my wife and son. Having a child does not put an end to marriage, but rather adds to it. Julie didn't stop being my wife and become the mother of my son. She is still my wife, but with the extra bonus of being my son's mom.

As a father, the best thing I can do for my son is to love

his mommy. My son needs to see his daddy communicate right with mommy. He needs to see daddy being faithful to his mommy. He needs to see his daddy kiss his mommy goodbye and tell her that he loves her. He needs to hear mommy talking on the phone with daddy and hear mommy say, "I love you too!"

Couples that put children before marriage face more problems than you can imagine. Children can discern where they fit in the pecking order. If a child senses that they can divide mother from father, they will try to use it for their own benefit. At their core however, children truly want their parents' marriage to be a solid union that no one can penetrate.

When couples get a divorce and there are children involved, one of the most common feelings felt by children is the feeling of guilt that perhaps they had something to do with their parents' split. Parents must often console their children and help them understand that the divorce was not their fault. This is additional evidence that children truly want and need their parents' marriage to be a priority.

Children need to know they are the priority of both parents together, not of each parent separately. A child should never have to be confronted with the question of who loves them more, mom or dad. This was the case for Jacob and Esau in the book of Genesis.[51] Isaac favored Esau while Rebecca favored Jacob. It caused a lot of problems and eventually led to Esau wanting to kill Jacob. It appears to have also caused division between Esau and Rebecca. Children need to see that they cannot come between their parents because their love for one another is so strong. Though they are loved individually by their parents, they view their parents as a unit; mom and dad.

Second marriages with children bring a completely different set of problems. The Brady Bunch blended family comes with its own set of baggage that the couple must figure out how to carry. Perhaps, you feel guilty for the pain you have put your children through by getting a divorce. Upon getting remarried, it is not uncommon to overcompensate and be overly protective of your child even from your new spouse. Some spouses will make rules with each other that the other spouse is not allowed to discipline their child. Perhaps there are demands from the ex-spouse which limit what the new spouse is allowed to do when disciplining the children. Having been burned in the first marriage, people tend to be more guarded in terms of children, money, and communication. If the divorce was the results of infidelity, you can bet there will be a tendency to be more suspicious.

I hope you are able to see the marriage killers waiting to assassinate the second marriage. Whether it is a first marriage or a fourth marriage, the pitfalls are the same, as are the remedies. Whether the children in your house are your biological children or not, they need to be raised and disciplined by a cohesive team consisting of a married man and woman. Even if it is a second marriage, all the children in the house need to see that the mother and father love each other first and together will make decisions; all decisions.

To use an analogy from the last chapter, there can never be more than one other person in the garden of your marriage. Sometimes it's a snake trying to get between you and your spouse. Sometimes it's your child.

COUPLE DISCUSSION QUESTIONS

Take some time to talk through the following questions. Allow equal time for both of you to talk and listen.

1) Do you want to have children? How many?

2) What are your beliefs regarding raising a child? What do you believe are appropriate ways to discipline a child?

3) How were you raised and how has the way your parents raised you affected the way you think about raising children?

4) How long would you like to be married before having children?

5) Why is it important for couples to parent as a team regardless of whether the children biologically belong to both of you?

6) What strengths do you possess that will make you a great parent? What strengths do your spouse possess that you will rely on to raise your children?

Struggling to Conceive

As I indicated in the last chapter, my wife and I took quite a while to conceive. We didn't have any way of knowing this would be a problem before we got married, but God knew and would provide us with an opportunity to show faithfulness to Him when it didn't appear to match our own desires for a child.

Fortunately for us, this is not a problem that lacks precedent among God's people. The inability to conceive is a dilemma faced by Sarah and Abraham, Isaac and Rebecca, and Jacob and Rachel. In each case we see their faithfulness to God tested by a profound desire to bear children in the midst of apparent infertility. Like them, our faith is tested and we are afforded the opportunity to prove our faithfulness to God if we face the struggle to conceive.

For Abraham and Sarah, having a child, and in particular a son, was a dream that had eluded them until age made such a hope impossible. Yet when God promised Abraham a son to be his heir and descendants as numerous as the stars in the sky, Abraham believed, and hope was rekindled that he would be a daddy.[48]

Sarah's response was to take matters into her own hands rather than trust God by seeking a surrogate mother to bear a child on her behalf.[49] The surrogate was Sarah's maidservant, Hagar and conception is accomplished by Sarah allowing her husband to sleep with her.

Though Sarah's plan to *help God* fulfill the promise He made to Abraham (that they would have a child), it would only lead to disaster and heartache. The child that would be produced by Abraham and Hagar would be Ishmael (from whom the Arabs come). When God eventually allows Sarah to conceive in her old age and she brings forth a child, they name him Isaac (from whom the Jews come). To this day the Arabs and Jews are in heated conflict and the origin is an improper response to infertility.

When Isaac grows up and eventually gets married, he too will have a problem of infertility with his wife Rebecca. Unlike his father Abraham, Isaac paints a clearer picture of a righteous response to not being able to conceive. Genesis 25:21 says,

"Isaac prayed to the LORD on behalf of his wife, because she was childless. The LORD answered his prayer, and his wife Rebekah became pregnant." [50]

Isaac recognizes that taking matters into his own hands will not accomplish God's will. Instead, he talks to the Lord about the problem and asks him to fix it. This is the way we are to handle problems which are outside of our control. The answer is never to commit sin to bring about the desires of our heart. When it comes to children, God controls the womb.

The inability to conceive is a dilemma faced by Sarah and Abraham, Isaac and Rebecca, and Jacob and Rachel. In each case we see their faithfulness to God tested by a profound desire to bear children in the midst of apparent infertility. Like them, our faith is tested and we are afforded the opportunity to prove our faithfulness to God if we face the struggle to conceive.

We are blessed today to have physicians and specialists that can help us increase fertility. Seeking help from physicians is not sinful or wrong. Bringing another woman in to your marriage for the sake of bringing about a child clearly is.

When Isaac and Rebecca conceived, they bore not one child, but twin boys. Their son Jacob would find himself in a marriage with two women at the same time; one he loved and another he did not. In Genesis chapter 29:31-30:24, we read the heartbreaking story of two women who appear to view children as the means of earning love from their husband. The account reveals the competitive nature of Leah and Rachel as they turn to giving their maidservants over to Jacob to create children. The children produced through this competitive procreation will become the twelve tribes of Israel.

The tragedy of the story, in my opinion, is not just the means taken to bring about these children, but the insatiable desire for love not felt by the women involved. How would the twelve tribes of Israel have been different had Leah or Rachel not felt that producing a child for their husband would make him love them?

You should never believe that having a child will make you love each other more. Children don't create love between a husband and a wife. Children are consumers of love already present. Many young girls have purposely gotten pregnant attempting to get a man to stay with her and many couples have had a child to fix the lack of love in their marriage.

The simplest way to avoid these pitfalls is to focus on one another and trust God that He will give you what is best for you. Psalm 37:4 say, *"Take delight in the LORD, and he will give you the desires of your heart."* Notice it doesn't say, trust in yourself to make your desires come true." Children are such an incredible gift. It is right for children to be the desire of your heart. But no child or spouse or anything else should ever be a greater delight than the Lord.

If you struggle to have children, it's okay to seek medical advice and use means consistent with honoring and delighting in the Lord. But scripture teaches our attitude should be one of dependance on God. We go to Him and prayer, trusting him with whatever outcome he wills.

COUPLE DISCUSSION QUESTIONS

Take some time to talk through the following questions. Allow equal time for both of you to talk and listen.

1) Do both of you desire to have children?

2) How would you feel if you were having difficulty conceiving?

3) What would you feel comfortable doing from a medical or scientific standpoint to have a child?

4) How do you believe such a struggle could affect your marriage? What would you expect from your spouse if infertility became an issue?

5) What are some other major struggles, besides infertility, that would be difficult for you to accept?

6) What is your view of children and their ability or inability to create love in a marriage?

IN-LAWS

There are some relationships that you get signed up for by default. Most of us have people we end up spending time with because they are friends of a friend or friends of a family member. You wouldn't choose to spend time with them, but because they are friends of your friend or family, you are willing to make the best of it.

When it comes to in-laws, we need to be a little more proactive. Friends of your friends and family can come and go, but your spouse isn't going to ditch their parents. When you choose to marry someone, you are also choosing to enter a special relationship with your spouse's mom and dad. The relationship you foster with your in-laws can be either a curse or a blessing and I want to help you do everything you can to make that relationship a blessing.

First, it is important to come at the in-law relationship with some perspective. Parents are used to having a significant say in their child's life. When someone else takes the position of the most influential, it can be hard for a parent to take. Likewise, it is natural for a daughter or son-in-law to not feel completely comfortable at a new family's holiday gatherings. After all, you are a newcomer to a holiday that has been going on for decades in your in-law's home.

> What your in-laws want more than anything is for their son or daughter to be happy in their marriage. If you continually show your parents that you are happy in your marriage, you will have little trouble.

Because this book is written for couples and not for in-laws, I will address the in-laws from the point of view of a couple. Fostering a positive relationship with your in-laws is rather simple. There are many strategies for blending into the family that we could discuss, but it would only complicate things. There are two things you should focus on to foster a good relationship with your spouse's parents. The first is this: What your in-laws want more than anything is for their son or daughter to be happy in their marriage. If you continually show your parents that you are happy in your marriage, you will have little trouble.

Second, your spouse's parents want to continue to have a significant voice in their son or daughter's life. That doesn't mean that their voice needs to be louder than yours. It just means that they want to continue to have a free and healthy relationship with him or her. As the son or daughter-in-law, encouraging that growing relationship with your spouse and his or her parents is important.

Finally, your spouse's parents want to know that you respect them. By appreciating them for the spouse they raised for you, you will earn respect in return. Your spouse's parents can become great advocates for you and your spouse, encouragers in your marriage and allies as you face the trials of life. Fostering this relationship will be of great value to both you and your spouse for many years to come.

Though it may be a bit uncomfortable at first, you can have a rich and special relationship with your spouse's parents. Over time you may well grow to love them like they are your own parents. And believe it or not, they may actually love you like you are their own son or daughter. Don't be surprised when you find out your mom has been on the phone with your wife for an hour while you were gone or your dad went golfing with your husband without you. Begin to see all your parents as "our parents". Love them like they are your own and be blessed by the results.

COUPLE DISCUSSION QUESTIONS

Take some time to talk through the following questions. Allow equal time for both of you to talk and listen.

1) How do you feel about your fiancé's parents?

2) How do your parents feel about your future spouse?

3) How can you both communicate to your parents that you are happy in your marriage?

4) What are areas of your life that your parents will want to have a voice in?

5) How will you address situations where your in-laws don't agree with you or your spouse? What if they are suggesting something different to your spouse than you?

6) What do you have in common with your spouse's parents that could be a means of drawing you closer?

The End of Marriage

On your wedding day you will be pronounced husband and wife and your married life will finally begin. But let's be very clear with each other. All marriages end. As believers, we wait in expectation of the return of Jesus to get his bride, the church. If you are alive on Earth when that happens, your marriage will end at that point. Matthew 22:30 says,

"At the resurrection people will neither marry nor be given in marriage; they will be like the angels in heaven."

Yet other marriages will end when a spouse dies. The wedding vows you take say, "until death do us part." We vow that our marriage will come to an end at a very specific time and that time is when either you or your spouse dies.

But just because you will no longer be married in the same way you were when on this side of heaven doesn't mean that your relationship with your future spouse will be over or be less intimate than it was on Earth. I agree with Spenser Thomas Creech who writes,

> If earthly marriages are a fallen image of the perfect marriage between Christ and His church, it stands to reason that this fallenness will manifest itself in earthly marriages that are less than perfect.

"The couple will know each other in better and deeper ways, and they will have so much more time to spend together than they had on earth."[46]

In heaven, we will be free from all that sin has marred in this life, which includes much that hinders and limits our ability to intimately know and love another person. Indeed, your relationship with your soon to be spouse will be infinitely better when it is upgraded from an earthly marriage to a heavenly eternal friendship.

Still other marriages will end because one or both in the marriage choose to end it. Though marriage is a lifelong commitment made with a vow, that does not mean they will all last a lifetime. If earthly marriages are a fallen image of the perfect marriage between Christ and His church, it stands to reason that this fallenness will manifest itself in earthly marriages that are less than perfect. We will see earthly marriages that lack love unlike the perfect marriage it points too. We will see earthly marriages that are unfaithful, though Christ is always faithful to His church. We will have men and women that abuse and hurt one another, though Christ always protects like a shepherd caring for his sheep. And though Christ will never leave you nor forsake you, fallen people this side of heaven will leave one another. Marriage on Earth is not equivalent to marriage in heaven. It simply attempts to draw our eyes to the perfection found in the relationship between Christ and His church.

There is, and has only ever been, one answer to the sin of men and women. We have never been able to live up to the holy standards of God. The answer has always been the grace of God. Grace is God's unmerited favor. God treats us well when we don't deserve to be treated well. God stays in a marriage relationship with his bride (the church) though she is unfaithful to Him. (Read the book of Hosea to see the comparison between God and His people in this relationship).

Dr. Beth Felker Jones, an Associate Professor of Theology at Wheaton College, is quoted in Christianity Today saying,

"Marriage, created by God as a "one flesh" union, is meant to be a sign of God's unbreakable covenant with us. This is an important symbol through the Scriptures: God is compared to a husband and God's people to a wife. When, by the grace of God, we're able to keep a marriage together, we get to be symbols – imperfect symbols, but still symbols-of God's faithfulness to his people. Marriages are supposed to last because they are symbols of God's lasting love for us."[47]

Though the church tends to judge it as so, longevity is not the only standard God sets for marriage. Is a marriage of 10 years that ends in divorce more sinful than a lifelong marriage filled with abuse and infidelity? Was the couple that stuck it out more righteous simply because they didn't succumb to the evangelical church's stigma sin of divorce? Which marriage is a more compelling symbol of God's marriage relationship with His church?

By no means am I diminishing the seriousness of marriage being a lifelong commitment. There are really, very few Biblical reasons for divorce. God's ultimate desire is for reconciliation, but sometimes that is not possible. Sin divides, Christ reconciles. Though forgiveness can be done on your own. Reconciliation requires two people. Reconciliation is not always possible this side of heaven.

If you are reading this book and have been divorced, know that you have not committed the unforgivable sin. There is grace and forgiveness in Christ. If you are re-marrying, take seriously the opportunity afforded you to be a symbol of God's faithfulness to his people by working hard to make your new marriage last.

COUPLE DISCUSSION QUESTIONS

Take some time to talk through the following questions. Allow equal time for both of you to talk and listen.

1) Have either of you ever been married before? If so, what were the circumstances that led to the divorce? Do you believe you had a Biblical reason for divorce?

2) Read Matthew 19:1-15. What does this say to you about divorce? What stands out to you as key parts of the verse?

3) Read Matthew 10:21-23. Does this give us any insight into what God thinks is appropriate when facing persecution (abuse)?

4) Read 1 Corinthians 7:1-16. What does this teach us about married life?

5) Do you think your relationship with your fiancé will be even better once you are both with Christ? Does it matter that you will no longer be married to each other in heaven?

Footnotes

1. Genesis 2:18 (NIV)
2. Genesis 2:20b-25 (NIV)
3. Genesis 2:18 (NIV)
4. Genesis 2:24 (NIV)
5. Pope, Jenna, The First Century Jewish Custom of a Groom Proposing With a Cup of Wine. http://www.ehow.com/info_8626993_firstcentur ygroom-proposing-cup-wine.html
6. Luke 22:20 (NIV)
7. Romans 6:23 (NIV)
8. Ephesians 5:25-27 (NIV)
9. Ephesians 5:27 (NIV)
10. Matthew 1:18-19 (NIV)
11. "The Ancient Jewish Wedding and the Return of our Bridegroom King" www.opendoorministrie swv.org/ancientjewishwedding.html
12. John 14:2-3 (NIV)
13. Matthew 25:1-13 (NIV)
14. Matthew 24:36 (NIV)
15. Revelation 19:6-9 (NIV)
16. Ephesians 5:25-27 (NIV)
17. Ephesians 5:25 (NIV)
18. Romans 3:23 (NIV)
19. John 17:9-12 (NIV)
20. John 18:8-9 (NIV)

21. John 10:11-15 (NIV)
22. Joshua 1:5 (NIV)
23. Exodus 16:12-14 (NIV)
24. John 2:1-12 (NIV)
25. The feeding of the five thousand can be found in Matthew 14:13-21 (NIV)
26. John 4:19 (NIV).
27. Exodus 20:3 (NIV)
28. Genesis 4:27-28 (NIV)
29. Romans 1:24-27 (NIV)
30. Romans 1:27 (NIV)
31. 1 Corinthians 13:4-13 (NIV)
32. John 14:15 (NIV)
33. 1 Corinthians 13:4 (NIV)
34. John 4:8; 1 John 4:16
35. 1 Corinthians 10:17 (NIV)
36. Ezekiel 28:17
37. 1 Corinthians 13:6 (NIV)
38. 1 Corinthians 13:7 (NIV)
39. 1 Corinthians 13: 7b (NIV)
40. Genesis 1:28 (NIV)
41. http://en.wikipedia.org/wiki/The_Da_Vinci_Code
42. Ephesians 5:25-27 (NIV)
43. https://discoverthebook.org/i-go-to-prepare-a-place/
44. https://www.gotquestions.org/marriage-constitutes.html
45. https://carm.org/about-marriage/were-adam-and-eve-married-in-the-garden-of-eden/
46. https://www.theodysseyonline.com/what-will-

happen-marriage-heaven
47. Quote of Beth Felker Jones, Associate Professor of Theology at Wheaton College quoted in an article by Rebecca Florence Miller – April 27, 2016 "When Does the Bible Allow Divorce?" Scripture's guidance for broken, hurting marriages. https://www.christianitytoday.com/ct/2016/april-web-only/when-does-bible-allow-divorce.html
48. Genesis 15:4-5 (NIV)
49. Genesis 16:1-4 (NIV)
50. Genesis 25:21 (NIV)
51. See Genesis 27.

Bibliography

- http://en.wikipedia.org/wiki/The_Da_Vinci_Code
- Pope, Jenna, The First Century Jewish Custom of a Groom Proposing With a Cup of Wine. http://www.ehow.com/info_8626993_firstcenturygroom-proposing-cup-wine.html
- "The Ancient Jewish Wedding and the Return of our Bridegroom King" www.opendoorministrieswv.org/ancientjewishwedding.html
- The Holy Bible, New International Version [Grand Rapids, Michigan] Zondervan, 1973, 1978, 1984 by International Bible Society.
- Quote of Beth Felker Jones, Associate Professor of Theology at Wheaton College quoted in an article by Rebecca Florence Miller – April 27, 2016 "When Does the Bible Allow Divorce?" Scripture's guidance for broken, hurting marriages. https://www.christianitytoday.com/ct/2016/april-web-only/when-does-bible-allow-divorce.html
- Matt Slick - Mar 12, 2015; https://carm.org/about-marriage/were-adam-and-eve-married-in-the-garden-of-eden/
- Discover the Book Ministries; https://discoverthebook.org/i-go-to-prepare-a-place/
- https://www.gotquestions.org/marriage-constitutes.html

About The Author

Dustin Largent has been in pastoral ministry since 1997 and has officiated a great number of weddings over his career. He has been married to his wife Julie for over twenty years. An alumnus of Wheaton College, he is pastoring in Illinois after over 20 years of ministry in the Seattle, WA area. Dustin is also the author of "In Their Own Words - First Person Narratives from the Book of Genesis".

Made in United States
Orlando, FL
28 April 2025

60836550R00068